TO CLIMB A MOUNTAIN

The Life of A Young Pioneer

Florence Conway

To Climb A Mountain
The life of A Young Pioneer

© Copyright 2011 by the National Spiritual Assembly
of the Bahá'ís of Australia Incorporated

All Rights Reserved
Published by Bahá'í Publications Australia

ISBN: 978 1 876322 71 7

Email: bds@bahai.org.au
www.bahaibooks.com.au

Cover Photograph by: Qi Jie Oh
Cover Design & Book Layout: Massoud Tahzib

DEDICATION

To the Bahá'í youth of the world during this historic 5-Year Plan and to the memory of Ama-t'ul-Bahá Ruhiyyih Khanum

PREFACE

"Their bodies may linger on earth but their spirits travel in the immensity of space."

SWA p202

This book, a tribute to my son Mike's memory, is long in the making but was always a goal in the depths of my heart. Inspired by the quality of his young Bahá'í life and his mature dedication to his Faith which emerged during the dramatic social changes of the volatile "60s," I realized Mike's story might be one that needed to be shared with the Bahá'í youth of today. Thinking about writing it was not easy—my son was killed at the age of nineteen while pioneering in Denmark. Being a private person in many ways, I would have chosen to keep my personal loss safe in the recesses of my heart, never to be exposed to the scrutiny of a sometimes cruel world. Then a few years ago, two of my children, Bill and Topaz, asked if I would write about their brother's life. This spurred me on to fulfill a much earlier request voiced on two separate occasions by Ruhiyyih Khanum, urging me to write the story as an inspiration to other youth. For a long time it was too painful for me to return to the circumstances of that time. The task has not become easier, but it is late, and in my love and admiration for the Bahá'í youth of today, I have found the strength, courage, and determination to return to that time.

INTRODUCTION

There was once a boy, my son, who soared to the heights of spiritual joy, whose life inspired me but left me in wonder and awe. Always he seemed to hold a secret which he could not share. Always he was eager to move instantly and deliberately as though he knew that time was a rare and limited commodity and that he had to experience all of life so he could learn its important lessons. In his first experience on the ski slopes, for instance, he went to the very top and without a pause surrendered himself bird-like to the natural forces bearing on his young body to carry it to the bottom of the mountain. He made it safely, much to the relief of his mother to whom he related the experience later on returning home.

Mike was a child of the 60's and shared with that generation a fearless exploration beyond the limits of established thinking, a kind of spiritual rebellion against the materialistic goals of western civilization at that time. These were the flower children who spurned violence with the more powerful force of love. The spirit of that age allowed someone like Mike to bring forth his inner self like a butterfly released from its cocoon. Talk of God became the norm; interest in the transcendent was shared openly. It was difficult to put one's finger on any one indicator but it was certainly possible to feel the pulse of this new body of humanity. A blast of sunlight shone on a generation of youth, determined in not repeating the errors of their parents but at the same time lacking the guidance needed to channel its energy into a constructive force for the future.

With Mike, however, it was different. He was a Bahá'í, devoted to the goals of a new way of life which did provide guidance, a path of moral rectitude, and not only a vision of a future world of peace, but maybe more importantly, the means to achieve it. Within the youth of the Bahá'í community one could see the same departure from the values of previous generations but with the exhilarating addition of a firm sense of direction and purpose. They did talk freely of love and God and openly dedicated their lives to changing a tired and ailing world. This was Mike's generation. He embraced his place in history, adopted the direction laid out before him and wholeheartedly set about refining his values, perfecting his character and serving mankind in whatever way he could. It would not be an easy journey for Mike but with a radiant spirit he accepted the hurdles along his path.

Early on Mike learned about suffering, taking it in as the inevitable food for his soul, digesting it and growing from it. Never had I witnessed such resignation to the inevitable, such an ability to maintain an undiminished spirit in the face of severely limited physical energy. He never complained, but the heart of his mother perpetually ached with silent pain during those periods of his suffering. Yet, I rejoiced too at his victories of rising above life's difficulties and scaling the heights of dedication to the service of the Cause of Bahá'u'lláh to which he had committed himself.

1

THE CHANGES AND CHANCES OF THIS WORLD

As I look back on Mike's life it becomes easier from this vantage point to see a pattern unfolding from the very beginning. He entered the world on September 3rd, 1950 in a little hospital in Ashland, Ohio, surviving a traumatic birth that resulted from a nurse not having the good sense to let him arrive when he was ready, just because a doctor was not present. Later, all the discomfort from the painful stitches resulting from an unnatural forceps delivery melted away in the warm ecstasy of beholding this little human being all intact and so alive. Mike was round with full cheeks and alert eyes and of course I was instantly in love with the tiny creature.

When Mike was still under a year old an incident occurred which could have changed completely the future of our little family. It was a Saturday afternoon during an extreme cold snap in the middle of an Ohio winter. My head pounded – a different pain from my occasional headaches. I also felt drowsy and had trouble staying awake. Outside reigned the quiet of a heavy snow muffling the usual noises. My husband, Bill, was out trudging through the deep snow pulling on a sled two round, snugly-wrapped children, Mike and his older brother, Pat. They had been out for about an hour and were heading toward the back door with pink blooming cheeks and dancing eyes.

Later they had been fed, bathed, had their stories read to them and were tucked into bed. I had forced my body to accomplish these tasks then sank into a chair. Bill was also complaining about feeling tired and decided to turn in early. We were no sooner in bed and dropping off to sleep than sounds from the next room roused me. Rushing in I found Mike had thrown up in his cot. I cleaned him up, settled him down then went back to my own bed. A few minutes later I heard crying from Pat and dragged myself out of bed to see what had happened. He, too, had been sick to his stomach.

As I changed his bedding and pajamas a thought leapt out of my sluggish mind. Something was wrong. The only thing I could think of was a gas floor furnace which we used to heat our tiny apartment on the first floor of our building. I roused my husband who had been sleeping heavily and told him my suspicions. The first thing we did was turn off the furnace, then open doors and windows. Outside the temperature was about 10 below 0 (F). Within minutes frigid air was flooding into the house. I put more blankets on the boys and phoned the landlady who lived in the house next door. There was no argument about my suspicions and she brought us more blankets to get us through the night. After the airing we closed the windows and turned on the oven of our cook stove for awhile just to ease the frigid temperature, then went back to bed.

The next day repairmen came to inspect the heater and found the exhaust pipe full of holes from rusting. Beyond that, they found a rat had crawled into the pipe from the outside obviously seeking warmth from the severe cold. It had been overcome by the carbon monoxide and died. This blocked the exit of whatever deadly fumes could have escaped, and all of it instead had been backing up into out living quarters. We were told how fortunate we were in that children usually get sick before being overcome whereas adults just go to sleep and that's it.

It was a sobering experience for us and the consciousness of the tenuous nature of this life haunted me for years afterward. All that I knew and cared for could have been swept away in a few hours – a fall into nothingness, the blackness of no future vision, the common denominator for young parents with little children. I no longer was able to take life for granted. The unexpected twist in the road ahead could present a real threat.

2

THE BAHÁ'Í FAITH

Perhaps it was a good thing in that it prompted me to re-visit the old question about the meaning of life. The question had plagued me in previous years but lately it had been easy to put it aside. The distractions were there – total occupation with the needs of two small children, cultivating new friendships, adjusting to new places and struggling to get by financially on the meager income from my husband's teaching position.

In an attempt to find something meaningful that we could teach our children we tried to restore our lapsed Catholic Faith, but to no avail. I had grown up a devout Catholic, but a questioning adolescence had gradually eroded a belief system which to me did not make sense. A couple of years earlier we had come across the Bahá'í Faith while we were living in Evanston, Illinois. Its magnificent House of Worship was close by so we had visited this nine-sided structure with its lacework of concrete and quartz that shimmered in the sun as it looked over Lake Michigan. We had been given a tour along with some history of the Bahá'í Faith.

The experience was tucked away in my memory so when our weekly attempts to endure Catholic Mass led only to frustration I decided to write to the Bahá'ís in Wilmette, Illinois for more information. In all fairness, much of the frustration was the result of a very conservative priest who preached a literal interpretation of the gospels. Inquiring, rational minds like ours refused to even consider, for instance, the physical resurrection of all the dead bodies from the cemeteries at the 'time of the end', which the local priest taught and even had pictures depicting such a macabre event.

We soon received literature from the Bahá'í Center which spelled out principles which made sense and attracted our inquiring minds. So, from then on, even though we would not officially become members of the Faith until later, its basic teachings became the foundation of what we taught our children – that there is only one God, that all religions must have good within them since they all come from the same source, and also, that humankind is all one family. Our simple creed at least laid a useful foundation on which to build.

3

GROWING UP IN ANAHEIM

In Mike's first year of life we set out from Ohio and moved our family to California where my mother and stepfather already lived. We settled in Santa Ana, which was at that time a small self-contained town with tree-lined streets, and surrounded by vast orange groves. The children settled in well, enjoying the milder California climate. Since they were outside a great deal they got acquainted with our neighbors and would often go visiting with their wagon and car. Occasionally the peace of the neighborhood would be broken by loud, thunderous crying coming from Mike. It was the character of his voice at an early age that demanded that you drop everything and run to rescue him from some catastrophe. He was determined to be heard. Pat sometimes couldn't resist getting out some resentment for this relative newcomer to the family who was so captivating to everyone who met him. However, these outbursts would pass quickly and the boys were always the best of friends.

When Mike was about three years old, we bought a new house in Anaheim, not far away. It was a neighborhood full of children, young families like us with working fathers and stay-at-home mothers. Firm friendships were formed, some still extant almost 50 years later.

Mike's early allergies worsened in Anaheim until he began to have frequent asthma attacks. My heart was being torn to shreds watching this jubilant spirit being restrained by a weakening body. We sought all the medical expertise available at the time but nothing led to the complete relief I so longed for. We used everything from cortisone injections (which I gave him during severe attacks), to food eliminations from his diet to twice-weekly injections of antigens made from the substances he was found to be allergic to. Sometimes he would wake up in the middle of the night, barely able to breathe and we soon discovered that a quick trip to the desert would bring instant relief. So, on those nights, we would wrap him up and his father would drive to Palm Springs, rent a room at the Ranch Club where we were members and Mike would have complete relief. It was just the radical change from moist coastal air to the dry of the desert that eased his breathing.

Later when inhalers hit the market we got him one immediately although we were cautioned against his becoming too dependent on it. However, the important thing was that it offered him some control of his own condition.

Despite the pain and suffering, Mike had an incredible ability to accept the restrictions his health brought to his life, and was still able to enjoy, explore, and delight in and learn from his life. Before his health declined he was a vitally alive little creature. I can see him, taking a break from one of his many adventures, sitting in his car seat on the driveway with a cap tipped to one side of his head shading those insatiably joyous eyes, eating contentedly on some snack and occasionally laughing with his wonderful laugh that came from the depths of his being.

He still had that surprisingly powerful voice and used it effectively whenever he was unhappy with something his older brother did. It got immediate response. One day he was at the back door again crying at peak volume. That was the time I decided that my response had to change. I waited but he still wouldn't cut down the volume of his crying. Finally I gave in and went to the back door to find Mike with an obviously broken arm. He had climbed to the top of the gym set and fallen. Needless to say I was devastated and it took me longer to recover from the guilt I felt than it took Mike's arm to heal.

Mike's adventuresome climbing was not limited to the jungle gym but was also exercised within the house. His piggy bank had been put on the top

To Climb A Mountain

shelf of the linen closet to keep him from emptying it whenever he heard the tantalizing tune from the ice cream truck passing by. One day during his nap I took a breather and was on the back patio reading. Suddenly, some children's voices out front caught my attention. I first went into Mike's room and found the bed empty. I looked out the window and saw Mike with some of the neighborhood kids buying treats from the ice cream man. Mike had treated everyone. He had managed somehow to retrieve his bank from the top shelf and emptied it. An act of such expansive generosity had to go unpunished, with just a warning that climbing can sometimes lead to accidents. But his adventurousness sometimes led to other lessons.

One day, a couple of years later Mike arrived home from school saying he had gone to the supermarket with his friend, Mark. Before long, word reached me through Mark's mother that they had taken some candy from the store. I confronted Mike and he said it was true. He showed me the candy. I talked to him about the importance of honesty (although he always told me the truth) and that this was really stealing, and that he should go back to the store and apologize to the manager and return the candy. He sensed the gravity of the occasion and headed back to the store. In the meantime I phoned the manager and told him Mike was on the way and that he should use the experience to quell any future tendencies on the part of my little adventurer toward a life of crime. Mike returned home later visibly shaken by the experience. The manager outdid himself and told Mike that he was lucky this time around and oftentimes when people steal the police take them to jail. It was the end of any inclination that Mike might have had to transgress the law. The manager might have gone a bit too far but Mike completely absorbed this lesson about the need to be honest and trustworthy.

Eventually Mike's body began to show the degenerating effect of the energy drain behind every breath. By the time he was about eight years old, his asthma had become chronic. One day I realized with shock that it had been months since I had seen him run. When he was able he would walk to school and at the end of the day just seemed to have enough energy to get home and that was all he could manage. Gradually the healthy body and the dear round cheeks began to fade. Dark circles shaded the formerly life-filled eyes. To watch this process take place gives me extreme pain even now remembering those years watching one of my children suffer so much. I tried to conceal my pain from Mike because he had gradually learned to live with his handicap since it had come on so early and slowly. He figured it was just part of his life and never complained. He just adapted his pace of life to cope with his energy level at the time.

The pattern seemed to be set as Mike moved on to various crises always followed by a victory of his indomitable spirit. He was driven toward some destiny which I could not then understand.

It was clear that Mike loved animals and he soon asked for a pet. A dog or cat was then out of the question with his severe asthma so we got him a baby chick. His Dad built a little cage for it in the backyard and Mike lovingly cared for it. One morning I awoke with some trepidation on hearing something that sounded too much like a crowing rooster. It seemed our little chick was indeed a male. Our next door neighbors complained loudly and the woman told us it was waking her husband every morning and it had to go. It was a fair complaint albeit delivered with too much hostility. I consulted with Mike and told him that we probably would be unable to keep the rooster, but there was a place we could have it "dressed" for eating. Mike thought for a minute, knowing instantly that we could not eat it, then suggested we give the "dressed" chicken as a gift to our neighbors who had complained. I was stunned but pleased at this gesture of kindness from him (although I thought I detected a slight trace of playfulness lurking in those twinkling eyes). In any case we all agreed. A day or so later, Mike delivered the dressed 'pet' to the people next door. They were so shocked they were unable to even thank him.

Since this incident left Mike again without a pet we re-visited that void in his life. He asked if snakes would affect his allergies. I swallowed hard and hid a creeping dread, and said probably not. The other children, now four in all with the addition of his sister, Topaz, and brother, Bill Jr. agreed that this would be fine with them. Pat's assent was most important since he and Mike shared the same room.

So off went Mike with his father to the pet shop and they returned with two snakes –a black racer and a smaller garter snake. Very gradually all of us learned to live with Oscar, the black racer, and Sam, the garter snake, in the house. They had a proper living space in the boys' bedroom with food and a good natural environment. My only requirement was that when we had guests in the house the snakes were to be kept in their own little 'house'. This worked out okay most of the time. However, one day I was entertaining a couple of friends and Mike came bounding into the living room.

"Mom, Oscar's out." I cringed and tried to dismiss him. The inevitable question came from one of the visitors, "Who's Oscar?" Mike didn't wait for me to give an elusive reply but blurted out 'my snake'. Legs were lifted from the floor, then on second thought, bums from the couch. Excuses were given that they had forgotten they had to be some place else and within seconds my guests were gone. Just as well because we found Oscar lurking under the couch where they had been sitting. The word must have gotten around for we now had a sudden dearth of visitors. Eventually, both snakes escaped not to return. Mike accepted the loss of these pets with the same acquiescence shown earlier, perhaps with a little more joy since he saw their possible escape to a nearby cemetery as a welcome liberation for them.

We had by that time enrolled as Bahá'ís and started having children's classes at our home every Sunday. Parents also came along and eventually it was quite a crowd and every room of our little house was used for one class or another. It was a poorly-structured effort compared to what we now have in our Bahá'í communities but it was a beginning and we established this foundation in Anaheim.

Since we have Bahá'ís of all races and nationalities, occasionally we had African American friends in our home from a nearby community. This served to agitate our neighbors even more than the rooster had. Again the woman came to see me and said that she could not be responsible for what her husband might do if we continued to have black people in our home. We had a family consultation and talked about the importance of sticking to our principles and not letting fear make us deviate. I told the children that they would probably be shunned by the family next door but they all agreed that it was more important for us to continue having our friends over to the house no matter what color their skin. Keep in mind that we were living in a small conservative town in the heart of the influence of a very conservative political movement called the John Birch Society. Only later did Anaheim grow to a more liberal, good-sized city, partly because of Disneyland.

So, we continued to have our friends, some white, some black, and other people of colour. The neighbors stopped speaking to us but we continued to greet them whenever we met. The part that made it a more bitter pill for the children to swallow was that those same people had a swimming pool put in at that time and all during the hot summer would invite all the neighborhood children except ours for swims. One day I found Mike at the top of the gym set (again) looking over the fence at all his friends enjoying the pool. However, none of our children ever complained about the decision we had made.

As Bahá'ís we were growing in our understanding of being a part of a world community and gradually boundaries were melting away. We realized that what skills we had could be used to more advantage in developing countries. We were motivated to 'pioneer' to another country since this is the way the Bahá'í Faith grows, through individuals' sharing it with others. Since there are no clergy in the Faith everyone becomes a teacher.

Africa seemed to beckon – a continent we knew little about except that it had been so dear to the heart of Shoghi Effendi, the late great-grandson of Bahá'u'lláh and the appointed Guardian of the Faith who loved the 'pure-hearted Africans'. We found out about a program jointly sponsored by Columbia University and the government of the United Kingdom in cooperation with the governments of East Africa to provide sorely-needed secondary teachers for Uganda, Kenya, as well as Tanganyika and the island of Zanzibar (the latter two now united to form Tanzania).

Mike's health was a concern so I consulted his specialist and asked him what he thought of the possibility of our going to East Africa. He said the change of climate might prove very good for Mike and suggested we go on this adventure. We applied, were interviewed, given a raft of psychological tests and were invited to go. In 1960 it was not a common thing for a young family of six to pull up stakes and move to the developing world—friends and family alike questioned our decision. To check out this phenomenon, the local newspaper sent a reporter and photographer to interview and photograph us. I think only our difficult neighbor might have rejoiced at the news.

My husband left early for orientation at Columbia University in New York, and then on to Kampala, Uganda where local Bahá'ís helped him to settle in. Shortly after his arrival, Bill ruptured his Achilles tendon and ended up with his lower leg in a cast and hobbling around on crutches. My hatching plan for a long slow trip for the rest of us by freighter to East Africa therefore had to be scrapped, although I desperately needed a break after packing our belongings, selling our house, furniture, and car, and winding up necessary business affairs in order to leave.

Selling a house while it's occupied by four children was not easy but we worked out a system. Since it was on 'open listing' it was possible for people to show up any time to take a look. Whenever a car pulled into the driveway I would go out onto the front porch to greet and delay our potential buyers as long as possible while the children swept up all their toys, shoved them under beds or in closets and appeared lined up and smiling like four little angels to greet our 'guests'. People would ask, "How do you manage to keep your house so clean and tidy with four children?' I would just look at the children proudly and shrug.

To Climb A Mountain

What could I say? Mike would always be standing there with an impish look in his eyes that swept across his beaming face.

We finally sold it, and the day came for us to leave the house they had all come to love, in fact the only one that Topaz and Bill, the two youngest, had ever known. We handed the keys to the new owners and left behind all our furniture, even the paintings on the walls. As we were driving away, I looked through the rear view mirror to see a pensive look on ten-year-old Mike's face. "We don't have a home anymore do we, Mom." It was a statement of fact and as he said it he drew closer to him the scruffy stuffed rabbit he had chosen as the one 'toy' he could take along with him. Again I saw in my child's face that acceptance that already characterized his meeting of life's challenges.

In the shipment we had sent earlier there were other personal belongings, as diverse as clothing to Mike's cherished bow and arrows, but in our luggage we had to find room for things like last minute tools and appliances (a hammer, screwdriver, iron, etc). Never would it be possible today to carry such things in hand luggage. It was necessary to distribute these items among carry-on pieces because of weight restrictions on our check-in baggage and comparative muscle mass of each of the children.

It was 1961 and our first airplane journey. What a joy flying was in those days – a sparsely occupied plane with lots of room between the rows of seats, room to move around or spread out for a nap and excellent attentive service. We stopped in Rome for a few days on the way. Keeping my children safe from the chaotic traffic occupied a good part of my energy. I located a pension where we got two adjoining rooms with sunlight pouring in and a chorus of voices floating up from the street below. The first night I decided to eat in at the little dining room of the establishment. The waiter did not speak much English and it was difficult to find something these Southern California children wanted to eat. In desperation I asked if they could just fix a hamburger and tried to explain what that was. Some time later the waiter returned with a large silver tray with a massive lid and ceremoniously uncovered it to reveal a miniscule patty of meat. Somehow we managed to satisfy our appetites with lots of bread.

The next day we met a young actor from Milan who was intrigued with the children, especially Mike who exuded a thirst for adventure, a ready smile and a natural interest in our new friend. Those were safer days and nothing opens up opportunities for conversation more than having four children trailing after you. He offered to help out if we wanted to go sightseeing and I enthusiastically accepted the kind offer. He took charge of a couple of the children while I took the other two and we were able to roam around without mishap in the hands of a 'local', covering so many of the lovely attractions in that beautiful city.

4

AFRICA

Our first stop in Africa was Khartoum, Sudan, and we disembarked so the plane could be re-fueled. It was early morning and a black storm cloud covered most of the sky except for the brilliant red strip along the horizon that signaled the approaching day. Shining black faces passed back and forth as they tended to their duties. It was all such a change from our home in Southern California. In silence I watched and I saw the dazzled eyes of my children taking it all in – an adventure to end all adventures.

We arrived in Entebbe, Uganda, our destination. After leaving the plane to walk the short distance to the terminal, my nostrils suddenly picked up all the pungent smells that pervaded the heavy humid air. I could see the children listing somewhat as they carried their heavy hand luggage. Inside the terminal we were met by their father, on crutches, his leg in a cast. Local Bahá'ís were there and pioneers Rex and Mary Collison and Ali Nakhjavani who would soon be leaving Uganda for Haifa, Israel to serve on the International Bahá'í Council, that body which was the precursor to the Universal House of Justice. This reception was like being enveloped in a loving embrace.

Some days later we were settled in a simple but adequate little house near the college where Bill would be teaching. It was outside the city of Kampala, (the largest city in Uganda, but small by most countries' standards). Pat and Mike shared a room and were soon able to unpack and organize their lives in the new environment. Mike savored the prospect of fresh and exciting experiences, being initiated a couple of days later by coming across a puff adder. His fearlessness of snakes now had to be tempered with a healthy respect for the many dangerous varieties that graced the African countryside. All the caution never seemed to curb Mike's race with time to experience all he could in life.

The children went to school in Kampala, catching the school bus each morning. Parents in the neighborhood took turns riding the bus with the children, just to maintain order. Mike's sense of fun encouraged him to use the otherwise boring bus rides as an opportunity to joke and play and sometimes perform harmless pranks. On one trip he was pursuing this habit but with an accompanying parent who seemed to lack any patience with children's antics. The woman stormed toward the back of the bus, and angrily confronted the first freckled face she saw, apparently remembering that facial characteristic of the offender. Unfortunately, it was the wrong freckled face and she struck young Bill, the sweetly innocent unlucky one. Neither of my children quite knew how to respond to this. They had always been taught to respect their elders so would not dare protest. They waited until they arrived home to tell me what had happened. Mike felt so badly that Bill had suffered the blame for his 'crime', and of course as a mother I was furious that someone would hit my child. I met with the woman that afternoon and strongly stated my position, that should my children ever misbehave she was not under any circumstances to physically punish them but to notify me.

The family of Hand of the Cause Musa Banani soon adopted us and became our main support, Mrs. Banani helping in the excursions for food, providing loving instruction as to how to prepare it all from 'scratch', and generally, taking us under her wing.

The resilience Mike had developed living with his asthma stood him in good stead in adapting to life in Africa. He settled in and I began to notice some improvement in his health. I noticed, too, that in relishing the challenges of life in a new country there emerged a growing independence and an increase in what was already an abundance of courage. One night, my husband and I decided to go into Kampala for a movie. We left Pat in charge and alerted Hamisi, our houseman, who lived at the rear of our house that we would be gone for a couple of hours and asked him to keep an eye on things. The other children had gone to bed and Pat was up doing homework. Suddenly he heard a noise coming from our bedroom and went quietly to the doorway to see a long arm reaching through the bars on the window toward my jewelry box. The story we got was that Pat let out a yell, woke Mike, and went out the back door to get Hamisi. As he did, the robber went around the house in the opposite direction and ended up at our back door to find Mike standing with his bow drawn and an arrow ready to fly. The robber, obviously stunned, decided he should get away as quickly as possible. Hamisi and Pat showed up at the door seconds later and found all the children gathered there with Mike, clearly the hero of the night, but nevertheless a bit shaken by all that had happened.

We got home shortly afterward to find Hamisi and the children sitting around the living room and the story tumbled out, a little from each of them. We phoned the police and they came about an hour later. On the following day a reporter from the Uganda Argus, the country's main newspaper showed up wanting pictures of Mike and his bow and arrow. The next issue of the paper proudly showed on the front page a picture of Mike with his 'weapon' and his siblings with the accompanying headline "CHILDREN FOIL BURGLARY ATTEMPT – WITH A BOW AND ARROW".

Soon after we arrived in Uganda, Mike found a wonderful friend in his teacher, Gerry Mossom, who was also his scout leader. Gerry was a young man from Britain, about 30, married but with no children. He was one of those special people who loved all children and he seemed to take a particular interest in Mike. Gerry apparently sensed that Mike needed an adult male friend. (Unfortunately, my husband, maybe being a product of his time, had difficulty forming a warm relationship with any of his children.) Gerry and Mike became fast friends and spent a lot of time together. Gerry's big black Labrador, Rover, made up the third member of this inseparable group. Mike's health began to improve in that he became free of the chronic breathing difficulty. On occasion, however, he would go into a severe attack and a couple of times blacked out and ended up in the hospital. This kept his physical condition a bit tenuous.

Gerry and his wife had long before decided to return to England at the end of his current work contract. I inquired one day what he would do with Rover. He quietly said that he had planned to have Rover 'put down'. Mike spoke up and asked Gerry if he would leave Rover with him. It seemed that Mike's love for Rover had cancelled any allergic reaction to the dog. After giving it some thought, Gerry let us know that he would be happy to leave Rover with Mike providing that if we left Africa we would then have Rover put down. In East Africa at the time dogs were not cared for in the same way that Europeans cared for their animals. Mike agreed to do as Gerry asked and I said I would support the plan.

The time came when Gerry brought Rover to stay and shortly after that, the day of Gerry's departure. We went to see him off at the train station. There was a crowd, many of them former students of Gerry's. Our goodbyes were controlled but tearful. My heart was wrenching and all I could do was hope that Gerry could somehow sense my gratitude. This man had given so much love, care and time to Mike's life. I couldn't risk the words because I knew I would break down emotionally. Amidst the loud farewells I looked over at my son's face, trying to ascertain what lay behind those pensive eyes. Was it quiet resignation to the inevitable changes of life? A slight but warm smile crept over his face and I witnessed the momentary connection of two souls as I saw Gerry at the other end of that exchange. The moment passed and I knew the important goodbyes had been said earlier.

Within a few months of Gerry's departure I received news that he had suffered a massive heart attack and had died. He was only 32 years old and his wife was close to delivering their first child. The news shook me to the core and I could not imagine the effect it would have on Mike. I could not fully understand Mike's subdued response to the news. It almost seemed that Gerry's leaving had closed up a deep place in Mike's heart. It was as if it was not a surprise, that for him, Gerry's spirit had departed the day he left Kampala. On reflecting on this later I almost felt that this young child of mine already knew something about death that I had yet to learn. (Much later when Rover had to be put down on our departure from Africa, Mike would show the same inner strength that belied his young age.)

After Gerry left Africa, and with Rover at his side, Mike moved on to different things in his life and embarked on a new path of self-discovery. Never totally free of the effects of his asthma, Mike approached life with a certain urgency and total openness. His natural adventurousness was now combined with an abandon that came possibly from Gerry's passing. Even at such an early age he seemed to realize his own mortality, that life had to be lived quickly – this learning and experiencing. So, when the energy was there, he never held back. Unmistakably, here was a free spirit, not to be controlled by anyone and he was already approaching life with a full-blown relish. He had a keen curiosity and a delightful sense of fun which only his physical limitations kept in tow.

5

KILIMANJARO

In August, 1962 the mountain climbing club of the college where Bill was teaching, headed by experienced climber, Paul Latham, a British instructor and journalist, decided to take on the highest mountain in Africa, Kilimanjaro. The club had previously climbed other mountains, Mike and Pat joining them for one of their earlier climbs, Mt. Sabinio, one of a chain of volcanoes on the border of Uganda and the Congo.

The Kilimanjaro climb was the culmination of the previous climbs. Paul invited both of the boys on this adventure, but I was in doubt about letting Mike go. He was only eleven years old. Pat's school was still in session, so he couldn't go, but Mike was determined. His father finally persuaded me that he would take very good care to protect Mike from overextending a still frail young body and would turn back if Mike showed any sign of being in trouble. So one morning at 4:00 am, with packs on their backs and ice axes in hand, they joined the small group in the school van and departed.

To Climb A Mountain

After hours of driving they arrived in Moshi, at the foot of the mountain, and spent a couple of days gathering supplies and hiring porters for the trip. Here it must be said that climbing Kilimanjaro in those days was not what it is today. Few people did it, and at least this rag-tag group was very poorly equipped -- no special clothing, just something warmer for the higher elevations. What equipment they had, such as goggles, was not in sufficient numbers for all the climbers. For the final assault equipment would have to be shared by having two separate parties going at different times.

Mike was troubled with asthma for the first two days of the climb but it then subsided as the group ascended to higher elevations. They stayed at successive huts each consecutive night and Mike gradually found it easier to breathe.

They eventually reached Mawenzi Hut at the base of one of the two peaks of the great mountain where they would spend a total of five days to adjust to the higher elevation. Most of them were sick at this elevation of 15,500 feet. A few days allowed the adjustment required and also a chance for Paul Latham and three of the African students to climb Mawenzi, the lower but the more difficult of the two peaks of Kilimanjaro. They succeeded, but only after some of the people from the base camp set out with torches as darkness fell to guide Latham and the students safely back.

To Climb A Mountain

Next came the assault of Kibo Peak, the highest point of Kilimanjaro and of the continent of Africa. The first party set out the next day across the saddle of the massive mountain to Kibo Hut for a few hours sleep before making the final assault of the peak. The party was made up of Paul Latham, Mike, his father, and Paul Mawenga, an African student at the college. After crossing the saddle they set out in the cold moonlight of early morning. They had to make their way to the peak, then back down to the Mawenzi camp before darkness fell that night. They trudged on silently in the darkness undoubtedly wondering at times why on earth they had come. Then the sun rose with all its forgiving splendor, and warmed them, and teased them on. Physically, Mike was not fit for such a venture, but having always lived with discomfort, he already had learned to rely on his invincible spirit. On, higher and higher he went into a strange world of cold contradicted by blazing sun and vibrant sky. Then further up to the timeless place – a bare island floating on an endless sea of clouds – always with only one driving thought in mind – to get to the top.

The last grueling slope of Kilimanjaro challenged every inch of his body, and tripped his feet with deep razor-sharp waves of ice. It was as if the invisible spirit of the mountain was weighing on him to keep him back, and each step taken became an unbelievable exertion. The young African student did not go on, perhaps sensibly asking himself why he should participate in this madness. He turned around and went back to base camp.

At one point Mike became sick but after a short rest recovered. Paul felt that the ascent might be too much for his small body but Mike insisted on continuing. His father sank from exhaustion onto a patch of snow, dropped off to sleep for a few minutes, and then forced himself up and on. Five paces, then resting, then two paces and resting. For hours the slow, broken pace went on. At times they thought they would not be able to take another step, but then seemed willing to die trying—nothing else seemed to matter in that world of remoteness. They became so resigned to the automatic lifting of one foot after the other that they became numb and yielded to the insanity of continuing on forever if necessary.

As the last few feet stretched before them, they were stirred by a faint breath of excitement. It hurt to swallow and they felt ill. The numbness left. They registered the strain of the last few steps more keenly than any taken previously. A small stone plaque lay mockingly in front of them – Gilman's Point. The limp figures dropped to the ground like rag dolls.

To Climb A Mountain

Gilman's Point was traditionally where most climbers stopped, but around the edge of the great crater and up another 450 feet is the highest point in Africa, Kaiser Wilhelm Spitz. Mike asked Paul if they could go on.

Bill wanted to sleep, leaving the party of two to head off around the edge of the crater. Paul Latham later wrote, "We plodded on fitfully with numerous rests, mainly for my benefit. The going is the worst I have ever known it to be, the frozen razor-blade snow never letting up. A long time later, in actual fact only an hour or so, we reach the tattered flags that mark the summit. I can think of no one I would rather be with than my present companion, an eleven-year old reaching 19,350 feet by his own efforts. Amazing." They rested a short time while Mike gazed in awe and wonder at what surrounded him. Paul took a photo of Mike before starting the long journey down.

They met Bill and wasted no time since they had to make it back to Mawenzi base camp before dark. Although exhausted, they were somewhat revived by the descent. At 7:00 PM, 28 hours after they had started out, three tired figures staggered into camp, just before total darkness shrouded the mountain. They were given hot tea and the porters observed the custom of weaving a crown of everlasting flowers for the victors. Mike's dirty face beamed. He had conquered the "big one".

The Uganda Argus subsequently ran a feature story on the climb with the picture of Mike at the top of Kaiser Wilhelm Spitz, "...the 11-year old, believed to be the youngest person ever to climb to the 19,350 FT roof of the continent." Years later that record would be broken. However, when one contemplates Mike's physical condition and the poorly-clad and ill-equipped way this crew got to the summit – without the far superior equipment that later climbers would have – the feat looms a lot larger.

I had driven for two days with the other children to the Kibo Hotel at the foot of the mountain to meet the climbers. I was standing at the reception desk in the evening and turned to see Mike walk into the lobby. My heart leapt inside my chest, with joy and relief. He looked on the point of collapse but when he saw me a faint smile swept across the familiar face. He had just walked 27 miles that day and was wet through from the rain. In all, the group had been on the mountain for ten days.

I relate this story because it exemplified the fortitude, determination and courage that characterized Mike's life, even at this early age, and his reaction to tests of the most severe conditions.

6

RETURNING TO AMERICA

The time came in 1963 when we decided to leave Africa for a combination of reasons, but mainly dealing with the children's education. We opted for a long trip home via ocean liner, leaving from Aden, and spending almost two months enroute. It was a fascinating journey, stopping at exotic places along the way. We toured Sri Lanka and the children bubbled with curiosity wherever we went, from watching the fishermen prepare their nets to seeing the sights and experiencing the smells and sounds of Colombo. We wandered through the narrow alleys of shops of all kinds in Bombay (now Mumbai) and negotiated our way among the bodies of the sleeping homeless in early morning. It was a new experience for my children to witness this kind of urban poverty.

Traveling on to Malaysia and Singapore, we got a taste of the flavor of southeast Asia. We would usually hire a car and a driver as guide to take us around. Later, the ship stopped at various ports in Australia and we viewed Sydney before it became the vast metropolitan city it is today.

To Climb A Mountain

We left the ship in New Zealand to have an extended camping trip around the country while our ship, the Arcadia, took time out for a cruise. It was during this trip that I noticed a strain beginning to appear in Mike's relationship with his father. I can't remember what particular circumstances led up to the appearance of the first sign of this disturbing development. Mike's spirit always soared above the limitations that tried to ground it and as he got older it seemed to be more and more of a problem for his father. The sadness of it all was that Mike was an extremely good child in the true sense of the word but his thoughts, his attitudes and his goals were totally his own.

We got through the few weeks remaining in our journey, stopping in Hawaii and Vancouver before docking at Long Beach, California. We were greeted by friends and family, and a member of the press who wanted an interview, mainly because of Mike's Kilimanjaro adventure.

Eventually, we settled in the foothills of the Sierra Nevada Mountains in California outside of the town of Mariposa and very close to Yosemite National Park. We went to this location for two reasons, mainly the elevation and the dry climate we thought would be good for Mike's health and, secondly, following the Africa experience, it would have been almost impossible for us to re-adjust to the Southern California lifestyle. We had learned the value of a simple life, and were keenly aware of the ravages of materialism that infected the mushrooming population of suburban Southern California.

The move was miraculous in improving Mike's health. Now fourteen years old, he began to grow into a healthy youth – strong and responsible. He and, in fact all the children, worked hard on what turned out to be our 'funny farm' with an assortment of animals which seemed to grow daily after our arrival in Mariposa. We lived on 47 acres of land and it seemed we were compelled to populate it. In time we were growing most of our fruit and vegetables, had our own Jersey cow for milk and cream, pigs, chickens, horses, ducks, a lamb called Charlie Brown, goats and a couple of beef cattle. This was in addition to two dogs, Cindy, a black Lab who replaced Rover in Mike's life, and his friend Tuffy (a mix of something and Australian dingo we were told), and an assortment of cats. To maintain all this took the hands of all six of us. With some help, we also put in a pond, dug a new leech field and septic tank (mainly Pat, Mike, and their father) which took many hours each day during our second summer there.

In addition to growing stronger physically, significantly, Mike began to explore the life of the spirit. His relationship with others clearly reflected the fruits of his spiritual growth. In high school, Mike did well and was highly respected by his teachers for his principled nature, which was also sensitive and caring. Two of his teachers privately related to me that if the Bahá'í Faith had nothing else going for it but my son, Mike, it would be enough for them to have a very high regard for the truth of our Faith. His high school friendships never distracted him from a seemingly pre-destined journey of the spirit. One of those young friends later wrote "Mike was my brother and I loved him. He will always be in my heart." He befriended those in whom he sensed a depth of interest in life or a personal need.

One such person was a woman who ran a little drive-in in town and was known throughout the small community as a very difficult person to work for. She was cranky, demanding and never seemed happy. Sometime during his last year in high school, Mike sought a job to try to pay for his personal expenses; the allowance he received for the many jobs he did at home was insufficient to cover the petrol costs which his father wanted him to pay when he used our pickup to go to the occasional activity at school at night. For some reason Mike felt that he wanted to work for this woman to see if he could renew her faith in people and to make her life a bit easier. I wondered at this strange child of mine but praised his intentions.

He applied for the job and was hired. He was always sure to turn up on time, to carry out all his assignments with efficiency and in a happy frame of mind. If she was behind in her work at the end of his shift he would stay and help her finish up her tasks. After a long time of his doing these simple things she began to trust him. This opened the door for Mike to release that joyful spirit that he had cautiously kept in check. Soon she began to laugh and they became an effective and comfortable team. Mike was so pleased to be able to bring some happiness into this woman's life. I remember one night when he came home from work he shared with me that Mrs _____ seemed so much more happy now. It was a success in his young life in his effort to bring joy to other souls. When it came time for him to leave town to begin university, he stopped by with a little gift for her and to say goodbye. He never shared exactly what she said to him but I could somehow guess.

The beautiful maturing of his spirit was linked to Mike's immersion in the Bahá'í Writings. While we lived in Mariposa he read, one by one, most of my Bahá'í books with his characteristic engagement and intentionality. He was like a sponge and what was so special for me is that he always loved to discuss his impressions and ideas. It usually happened in the kitchen where Mike would seek me out. Sometimes he would see me cleaning up following dinner and would leave his chair beside the fireplace where he had been reading and would come out to help and talk. I was reluctant sometimes to signal him when it was his turn to wash dishes since this evening time was the only time he had to read. When Mike read about Bahá'u'lláh's life and teachings, he was gradually transformed from an adventurous adolescent into a mature young man. He took to heart the qualities that the Teachings said were latent in all humanity and with his characteristic determination set about refining his outlook, his behavior, and his inner being.

As Mike matured and blossomed, difficulties increased with his father. In my talks with Mike, I would never undermine his father but instead would point out that in our spiritual growth it was essential to always protect our own integrity, never to let our attitudes or behavior be shaped by our reactions to others—that we should become initiators instead, and courageously act on our values no matter what. Mike was inspired by the example of Abdu'l-Baha and was increasingly able to detach himself from the frequent criticism coming from his father and carried out his responsibilities at home with no complaints. He consistently maintained a transcendent spirituality.

To Climb A Mountain

One morning Mike shared a dream he had had the night before. He had come in for breakfast after doing his morning chores and we were sitting at the kitchen table. He dreamt he had cebrated his marriage but it was a strange ceremony in that he was alone on a mountain top – no bride, no witnesses, just him. He puzzled over the dream -- the clarity of it and the intense significance that it left him with on awakening. The meaning eluded me as well so we let it drop.

In our talks with each other, we often discussed what the Writings said about the next world -- the eternal development of the soul and the relationship of the departed souls to those loved ones on this plane of existence. One day we got a bit carried away in what was really happy talk about these things and even established a little pact that whichever of us went first would try to communicate with the other soon afterward to let them know what it was like passing to the next world. We even set the time so the one left would be waiting for the message. This sounds strange but it was promised seriously because Mike really wanted this to happen. It was a joyful pact because we both regarded the next world as a step up from this one, like the baby leaving the womb of the mother to emerge to this vastly different world.

To Climb A Mountain

Observing Mike's qualities and his intense motivation to learn, I was determined that he have an opportunity to get together with other Bahá'ís. We were living in an isolated place and missed contact with our Bahá'í family. So whenever possible, I would take the children to summer school sessions at Geyserville School near Santa Rosa, north of San Francisco. This historic campus had been visited by many illustrious Bahá'ís, including Martha Root.

Another special opportunity occurred in 1967 with an Intercontinental Conference in Chicago. Somehow we managed to scrape together money for Mike to go. We had friends who kindly offered to share their hotel room with him. While there, Mike met Hand of the Cause Mr. Samandari who was one of the speakers. Along with some other youth he sat on the floor devouring every morsel that was so generously shared by this man of small physical stature but of giant spiritual station. When Mike returned home, he was radiant with an inner joy. But we found to our shock that in his excitement to pack for the trip he had forgotten to take extra socks so had worn the same ones every day of the conference. This circumstance became quite a subject of laughter to our friends who had so kindly let Mike sleep in their room despite the detraction from its freshness whenever he removed his shoes.

Mike's time in high school was nearing an end. With the competing demands of his job, ranch chores, and regular study of the Bahá'í teachings, his studies never occupied that sole place that brought top academic attainment. Nevertheless, his school work was consistently good and he qualified for a California State Scholarship. His choice of school was the University of the Pacific in Stockton, California. There was an innovative program at Callison, one of its colleges, and part of the program was to spend the second year in India. For Mike's graduation I gave him his own Bahá'í library with the basic books of the Writings that he loved so much.

On the day Mike was leaving for university, I had hoped that his father and I would both take our son to Stockton. For some reason which I never understood, his father chose not to go. I hugged Mike goodbye after delivering him to Callison and attending an orientation for parents. It was late as I drove the several hours' trip home. My heart weighed in my body with a heaviness that I thought would destroy me in reaction to the distance existing between father and son. At the same time I felt relief that Mike would now be free to make his own way and to grow.

Mike came home for weekends now and then and would often bring friends from university. It was lovely to see him relaxed and happy, but he would never come home again for anything more than a long weekend. He needed to keep his distance while he tried to come to terms with his relationship with his father.

As a result, Mike spent his first long break with some Bahá'í friends, a family who lived some distance away in the Central Valley. He managed to touch their lives in a very profound way during this time. The wife and mother of the young family he stayed with described how his visit affected them:

"Many times since Mike was with us last summer I've wanted to put into words the meaningful experience that it was to me to get to know Mike for those few weeks.

"Mike seemed always to have a special secret that made him smile so spontaneously and so often. I noticed this especially when he arrived here, I also noticed that when we talked there was an honesty that was both disturbing and exhilarating. He seemed to possess a beautiful combination of innocence and intuitive understanding beyond his years – it was disarming. We talked many times during his brief stay – about so many things, values, children, our experiences growing up and how everything relates to being a Bahá'í. It amazed me how freely we could talk and how

Mike could put into words things I had been struggling to understand for such a long time. Mike helped me very much – it's difficult to explain this – perhaps it is enough to say that we get locked into distinctive patterns and it takes God's love coming through a kind and pure soul like Mike to give us understanding. It was very significant that he came here when he did – as though events turned in a direction that otherwise would not have been realized. John and I love Mike, he is a dear friend, and truly as Gibran has said –'When you part from your friend...that which you love most in him is clearer in his absence...and let there be no purpose in friendship save the deepening of the spirit....' Mike gave us a deepening of spirit as Bahá'ís, husband and wife, as parents and as individuals – and he continues to assist us, his presence is very real to me."

7

CALLISON, UNIVERSITY OF THE PACIFIC

During his first year at Callison, Mike began his studies but also formed a Bahá'í Club to continue the activities begun the previous year by another Bahá'í student. As a result of his teaching work, one of Mike's professors became a Bahá'í that year as well.

In the Callison program, his second year at university was to be spent in India but that plan fell through. In addition to his required courses, Mike had taken an extra elective course, just out of interest. At exam time he concentrated on his regular courses and did well but had neglected the elective. The unfortunate outcome was that he lost his State Scholarship.

He sought employment during his summer break and got a job in San Francisco working in the warehouse of a fine furniture company. He rented an apartment from some Bahá'ís and spent the summer getting to know the generation of youth which had paved the way for change in the American society.

Mike continued to change too, and in a most profound way. He had reached a strength and maturity of spirit that led him to initiate a reconciliation with his father, knowing the emphasis Bahá'u'lláh places on honouring one's parents.

After quitting his job in Mariposa, Mike's father, Bill had registered at the University of Massachusetts to enter a doctoral program, and we had sold our 'funny farm' and moved to Amherst, Massachusetts.

Early during his working summer Mike wrote:

"Dear Mom and Dad,

I'm sincerely sorry I took so long to find the answers I was searching for in my life, regarding my relationship with you. Please forgive me (I'm always kind of slow at learning things like this). But nevertheless, I would like you to accept what small money I have sent because I know you probably need it now that you have moved and Dad is going to school. I will try to send more if I can."

In this same letter, Mike informed us that he had lost his state scholarship and would not be going to India. Understanding his own difficulty, he reached out to his father to try to assist him as a fellow student.

This gesture of Mike made me sad in a way because I knew we would manage financially, but it was his way of respecting the fact that his father had always put a lot of emphasis on money and the need for his children to learn that as well.

Earlier the following month Mike sent more money and in response to an exchange of telegrams regarding his state scholarship he wrote: "Thank you for being so concerned about me. I really don't deserve to have such good parents." Through the influence of Bahá'u'lláh, this young person had managed to transcend the family experiences he had so painfully endured. Mike even then knew that in order for his own spirit to soar he could not allow himself to be burdened with resentments. Another victory for him!

8

PIONEERING FOR THE NINE-YEAR PLAN

While Mike made plans to continue his schooling in the fall, at the same time he became aware that the Bahá'í community of the United States had a goal to send four pioneers to Denmark during the Nine-Year Plan. His overwhelming desire to serve impelled him forward. He discovered a school in Copenhagen that offered an interesting program. He applied and was accepted. He then wrote to the International Goals Committee of the National Spiritual Assembly of the United States, asking if he could be counted as one of the four pioneers to Denmark. The committee enthusiastically wrote back:

"We are delighted to receive your letter telling of your plans to go to Denmark. ...[Y]ou will find it an enjoyable place to study and pioneer. We commend you on your wonderful enthusiasm and spirit...Our loving thoughts and prayers will surround you. Let us hear from you as soon as you have an address ...We will want to know how you get along from time to time...."

The letter also offered guidance, addresses and a pioneering manual for Mike's perusal.

After completing his plans for the following year, he decided to go to Geyserville Bahá'í School for the last session. He had made arrangements with his sister, Topaz, to go together and also invited his Callison professor to accompany them. Ever placing himself in the path of service, Mike performed some needed maintenance at the school during that time, especially painting. Other youth at that session were similarly on fire with the Faith and to bring Bahá'u'lláh's message to others. A letter to us from Topaz reflects the vibrancy of the time and the atmosphere in which Mike was steeped: "Geyserville was <u>too</u> much. For half the week there were over 300 people there. During the week we had 12 declarations. It was so stimulating – in fact (you better sit down) I've decided to go pioneering to the South with two girls from Los Angeles this January."

Since the school loans Mike had had previously could not be applied to expenses for a school overseas, he wrote to us asking if we might be able to help him if he could not arrange the finances. However, the underlying message that came through was that he had dispelled any remaining traces of separation from either of his parents:

"If you can't [help financially], don't feel at all bad – please. You have really done so much for me already I'm ashamed to ask you for anything. If I don't go to school this fall you must believe me, I will not feel at all bad. I want to very much but only if it is God's will. If not I would like to leave the rotting city I am in and come home for at least a little while to live with you two as children and parents were made to live, in love and unity. I feel a need to establish communication with you both because now I realize how much we can have to offer each other. You with your true wisdom and me with my experiences in this generation of 'now-ness'. Living in San Francisco has been overwhelming in itself. I am anxious to tell you the things I have learned. Many things have happened to me that I would like to share with you. Praised be to God. If I don't go to Copenhagen, I will see you both in a very short while. I value the idea of being with you two again as highly as I do going to school or being given a million state scholarships. God has been very good to me."

I called Mike and told him that we were sending the money and asked him to phone me from Canada, where he had a stopover for a couple of hours on his way to Denmark. When he phoned after arriving in Canada, his voice conveyed enthusiasm and joy at the adventure before him. He related how he had rid himself of extra belongings which he didn't need and had fit all his essentials into one suitcase and a carryon—"a lot of that space is taken up by my Bahá'í books!" (I found out later that he had given his motorcycle to a man in San Francisco who had no transport to get to work every day.) I wished him well, conveyed my love and promised that I would pray for him every day. He had just turned 19. As I contemplate that, I wonder how I could not only have let him go but even enabled it to happen. But, as it seemed to become increasingly clear with Mike, he had a path to follow and it was unfolding before my eyes. Perhaps it was not really in my hands.

9

DENMARK

He arrived in Denmark early in September. He went directly to the school to announce his arrival and then visited the Bahá'í Centre in Copenhagen. He introduced himself to the Bahá'ís serving there, one of whom subsequently wrote: "We were much taken by his devotion and eagerness to serve Bahá'u'lláh. Next day he came back. He was happy, had some 'posters' made which he had put into news papers announcing a Bahá'í meeting" [he already had a little job delivering papers].

On September 17, he met with the National Spiritual Assembly of Denmark. They read some prayers together and "he was greatly moved." After consultation with the NSA, he offered to go anywhere in Denmark where he was most needed. Obviously his intended university studies became a lower priority when he learned that Copenhagen had quite a large community. However, a Bahá'í group had recently been established in Aarhus on the Jutland Peninsula so he offered to go there. A woman on the NSA who lived there offered him accommodation. He attended a meeting at the National Centre at which Mrs. Faizi, wife of Hand of the Cause A.Q. Faizi, was present and then left for Aarhus to establish himself. He planned to return to Copenhagen in the near future for a party planned in his honor on the 4th of October by the Danish youth of Copenhagen.

On arriving in Aarhus, he wrote to his sister, Topaz, who was then at University of the Pacific and was continuing the Bahá'í activities of the previous year when Mike was there. She wrote back: "....I'm glad to hear you made it OK and also glad to hear that you're not in Copenhagen but out in the country. That's where Bahá'ís are supposed to be."

She described her own longing to go pioneering during the next school term and my apprehension about this. She asked Mike "to try to encourage Mom and Dad to support [her] plan." (During that time there had been intensive teaching going on in the Deep South and there were many new Bahá'ís who greatly needed deepening on the teachings of the Faith.) "They are ready now – it may be too late next year. We have already passed up too many opportunities in the past to teach the Faith...I am praying that Bahá'u'lláh will open the door for me soon. ...But in the four months I'm here in Stockton I want to do my best to get the community going.... Stockton now has enough members for an Assembly so that is one step.

"Margie and I have gotten the Bahá'í Club re-activated and this weekend we're holding a fireside in Callison Lodge. Some Bahá'ís from Redwood City are coming to "speak". We're having another one in 2 weeks. There are many people very interested here. It's very exciting."

She passes on greetings from many friends, then goes on, "All my classes and all the books I am reading are so interesting and relative to everything that's happening....At first I felt that I was not needed in California. I was ready to quit and go South. But after classes started it got better and I know now that the experience will help me grow in many ways before I go in January. Just pray with me that Mom and Dad will realize the urgency for me to go...."

"We are so blessed to be able to pioneer. It says in the Writings that pioneering is the highest station of servitude. No other deed surpasses the greatness of the station – and no sacrifice is too great when sacrificed for the cause of God. But Abdu'l-Baha warns us that we must deepen constantly so that we can teach the Faith in its purest form. And <u>live the life, live the life</u>. We are so blessed to be living in this day – to be living so close to the time of the Prophet – to be among the first bearers of the new word of God. Imagine – we are the spiritual descendents of the Dawn Breakers. What a station! The only way we can show our thanks and worthiness of this station is by being a servant of God – an abdu'l-Baha. I am learning and growing so much. I know you are too. But, there is so much we don't know. We must strive to obtain this knowledge. It is all at our fingertips – right in the Writings of Baha'u'llah. I say prayers constantly for you and for all the blessed warriors of Baha'u'llah. Please say some for me so I may join your army. Please write too if you have time. I need to hear from you. Stay happy and strong. Deepest Bahá'í love, "

(Mike never received the above letter from his sister.)

Although he had only just arrived in Aarhus, and had only been in Denmark for a few weeks, Mike quickly set about a plan to proclaim the Faith at the local university. He wrote letters to professors in various departments offering to speak to classes about some aspect of Bahá'í teachings relating to their field. He also set a date for a fireside to be held at the home of the Bahá'ís where he was living. I came across his early drafts of these proclamation letters; they went like this:

"I have recently settled in Braband after studying in America at a University in California. What

I would like is to offer to speak in one of your classes on the topic 'The Bahá'í Faith.' The Founder of this Faith wrote over a hundred volumes on the problems afflicting our world today that offer solutions to many of these same problems. As a divine Physician He analyzed the social, political, economic and personal maladies present in our society and presented to the world at about the middle of the nineteenth century a God-given remedy." Another to a literature professor, after introducing himself, states, "I have an interest in literature and have recently discovered some, extremely enriching, in the field of religion..."

In a letter, dated September 31[st,] he wrote to a different professor:" I am a student from America now living in Brabrand. I would like to have the honor of talking with you at your convenience, about the new Faith I have come across in America. I felt you would be interested because it is so relevant to this age we are living in. The name, Bahá'í, means, follower of the Prophet Bahá'u'lláh. He came to Persia in 1853 where He taught and wrote over 100 volumes, some of which I have.... Some of His teachings are the Oneness of God, the fact that religions come to man in progressive Revelations, and the Spiritual reawakening needed in order to bring about a lasting world peace. He has written about the need for science and religion to agree and work together to support a flourishing society...."

He closed the letter by inviting the professor to write him and expressed the hope that they might get together to discuss the new Faith.

Mike wrote at least a dozen such letters, always proclaiming openly his faith as a Bahá'í and trying to relate his offer to give a presentation within the recipient's field of interest. Meanwhile, he scheduled a meeting at the University's Student Union for a date in October.

In order to prepare himself to more effectively teach, Mike immersed himself in the comprehensive history of the Faith written by Shoghi Effendi, *God Passes By*. He had read it once in high school a couple of years before, but was captivated enough by this masterpiece to re-read it again in Aarhus. After reading about Bahá'u'lláh's incarceration in the Prison at Akká he was intensely drawn to the place and wrote to the Universal House of Justice to ask permission to at least visit the prison if he could not go on a full pilgrimage.

"If it is only possible for me to enter Israel and visit the prison in Akka by waiting on the long list of presently waiting pilgrims, I will do so. Please sign me up if this is the case...However, I am requesting permission by the Universal House of Justice to allow me, your obedient servant, to enter the country of Israel to visit Akka. Please forgive me bothering you with such a small matter as I know you are very busy. It is only that I now feel ready and ripe to visit such a place as Akka and take full advantage of the visit so that I might become a better Bahá'í."

Later the House of Justice wrote and invited him to go on a full pilgrimage.

As I review Mike's letters I realize the supreme degree to which he was liberated to courageously speak out and share what he believed to be the life-saving message from God for this period in human history. He had studied Bahá'u'lláh's Writings and his soul was engraved with their power and truth. He was a believer in every sense of the word. He took the Faith very seriously, tried to guide his life according to its teachings, and was always confident he would be assisted in actions of service. At the same time, he experienced the full joy that such an assurance brought to him. Now those dancing eyes were fed by deeper springs. He moved with an undeviating sense of purpose. I realize that souls such as Mike soar in a realm that cannot be easily described in words because it does "transcend the murmur of syllables and sounds". I was Mike's physical and spiritual mother. But when he chose to answer the call of his spirit, he traveled independently, never again to be enfolded in or restricted by the embrace of a parent.

Once he was settled and embarked on his teaching plan he was ready to travel to Copenhagen for a weekend to attend the party the youth had planned in his honour. The National Spiritual Assembly would be meeting on that same weekend and had invited him to have lunch with them to see how he was doing. Over the previous week Mike had invited a couple of the local Bahá'ís to go to Copenhagen with him on that Friday, the 3rd[th] of October. Unfortunately, neither person was able to go.

All that is known about the time preceding that trip was that for two days Mike had fasted. During that time he had been deeply moved by his reading of *God Passes By*. Perhaps he had fasted for the success of his teaching effort, or, perhaps he simply longed to be in His presence and knew that fasting was one means of doing that – I don't know. On the afternoon of his departure, he broke his fast and bought a cake to share with the family he was living with. He went quite early to board the ship which would take him to Copenhagen. The ship departed around midnight and would arrive early the next morning. One of the Bahá'ís was supposed to meet his ship on its arrival Saturday morning, but came to the dock very late. Mike was nowhere to be found. He did not show up for his lunch appointment with the National Assembly, nor did he appear at the party the youth had planned.

At that point someone decided to report that he was missing to the police who dismissed the matter as not urgent. They suggested waiting to see if he appeared by the dates of the meetings he had planned. In time hospitals were checked in case he had had an accident, but to no avail. His father and I were unaware of all of this until I received a call about two weeks later from the International Goals Committee of the United States which had just been advised that Mike was missing.

Something had happened, coincidentally, on the same Friday evening that he had embarked for Copenhagen. I had a frightening and very vivid dream about Mike, in which I was frantically trying to make my way to the top of a mountain where I knew Mike was engaged in a battle of some kind. When I was part way up, hordes of people were descending the mountain and I realized that I might be too late. I asked about Mike and some people said to me, "He won!"—they seemed to be rejoicing in his victory. I continued to make my way to the summit against the crowds of others coming toward me. When I arrived I looked down to see Mike's body lying lifeless on the ground. There was no sign of injury, just a cut on his forehead. I was shocked into wakefulness and very worried. I related the story of my dream the following evening when five of the family sat around the dinner table.

On the following Monday morning a letter arrived from Mike, relieving the fears I had regarding my dream. It did not occur to me that the letter would have had to be mailed well before I had the dream to arrive on that day.

After finally learning that he was missing, his father and I phoned the police in Aarhus to see if they knew anything, which they did not. We then phoned the police in Copenhagen. However, they viewed his disappearance as a typical young person's taking off, perhaps on meeting a girl. I tried to explain that the young person in this case would not have done that. We talked to the family he was staying with and they had heard no news. It was clear that we would have to go to Denmark ourselves and look for Mike. We drove to Boston to get our passports renewed and booked a flight to Denmark. Later that day I found myself alone at home and in a state of despair, fearing the worst – that perhaps I would never find out what happened to Mike.

I uttered a prayer from the depths of my soul – one of those rare kind of prayers that because of its wholehearted intensity brings a certainty that God would hear. I surrendered myself totally and implored that I would find out what happened to my son. I prepared myself for his death and in my prayer vowed that I would be able to accept God's will. I was in a state of complete surrender. Suddenly before me was Mike's face, shining brilliantly and with a joyful radiance that was indescribable. The words came tumbling forth like a sweet stream of water, "Mom, I am so happy. I am okay and it is wonderful." That was all but I knew then that Mike had passed on to the next world. Later that same afternoon the doorbell rang and a telegram was handed to me. Mike's brother Bill was there at the time and Pat's young wife, Nancy. The telegram was from the State Department of the United States:

IT IS THIS DEPARTMENTS SAD DUTY INFORM YOU ACCORDING MESSAGE FROM AMERICAN EMBASSY COPENHAGEN, DENMARK A BODY BELIEVED TO BE MICHAEL CONWAY DISCOVERED OCTOBER 22 IN AARHUS BAY. PASSPORT OF CONWAY FOUND ON CORPSE BUT IDENTIFICATION DIFFICULT DUE LENGTH OF TIME IN WATER. AARHUS POLICE EXPECT POSITIVE IDENTIFICATION FROM GRETHA RASMUSSON. CAUSE OF DEATH NOT YET DETERMINED.

A sound came from the depths of my being that I cannot describe – deep, deep from within. A sound between a groan and a roar from a place I didn't know existed inside me. I did not cry, that was something reserved for lesser emotions. Even though at some level I had known that Mike was dead, the shock of actually reading the words drained me of all physical and mental strength and I sank to a chair. I moaned and rocked, feeling my own heart had been torn from my body. The sweet child I had so carefully nurtured and cherished was no longer to grace this physical world.

After some time I was able to regain my mental composure and an unnaturally heightened state of consciousness took over my whole being. What was happening may not have seemed real but it required a response. I took on the efficiency of an automaton in preparing telegrams and mailing lists, phoning family members to inform them, and packing for the inevitable journey to bury our son.

We arrived in Denmark and took the ferry to Aarhus the following day, arriving at the home of the family who had hosted Mike there. It was a strange experience to see those who had most recently been with Mike and to see the room where he had stayed. We set about the task of arranging Mike's funeral, spending one evening with the family selecting appropriate readings. I felt both energized and numb as we approached the visit to the funeral director, selecting a casket. Later we went to the police station to get as much information as possible about the circumstances of Mike's death.

When we questioned the police and painfully extracted details about how the body was found it was clear that Mike had met with foul play. Mike's body had been picked up in a trawler's net about 16 miles off shore. A miracle by any sense of the word since his body had been resting on the ocean floor. He had been placed head first inside his sleeping bag, his legs had been tied together with some kind of tape, his hands had obviously been secured by a necktie which had been used to bind his wrists together on his chest. Ropes were used to secure his small travel bag on his chest. The bag contained 48 pounds of rocks, obviously used to sink the body so it would not rise to the surface. There was no money, no clothes in his bag, just two small prayer books. His body had been in the water for nineteen days.

Mike's father and I had the funeral at a cemetery in Aarhus. It was a small gathering of the tiny local Bahá'í community and a couple of friends from Copenhagen. I could not believe that the body of my son lay in the simple wooden casket. As it was lowered into the ground I felt my heart sink with it. Lingering after others started wandering away, I whispered words from the New Testament, "this is my beloved son in whom I am well pleased."

Later a large group of Bahá'ís gathered for a memorial service in Copenhagen. The following day we left for home.

The reason for his murder has never emerged — whether it was a random act or an attack by a person or group who felt deeply threatened by the message of the Faith which he was sharing – is unknown.

As we examined the circumstances of his death, we became more convinced that his murder had the mark of a ritualistic killing. Mike possessed supreme courage and believed with every ounce of his being that the solution to mankind's problems lay in the teachings of this newest of the world religions. He would have openly related to any crew members or anyone else he met on the ship. Soon he would have broached the subject with them of the message he longed to share. In his innocence he would have exploited any opportunity since one never knows what heart may be receptive. Obviously he spoke to the wrong person or persons. What occurred in those couple of hours can only be surmised on the basis of what I knew of Mike and the condition of his body that was recovered from the ocean floor, with only his prayer books in the bag that was tied to his chest.

If Mike's murder had been the act of a particular sect of extremists, binding the Writings to his body would have been an attempt to desecrate them. What is certain, however, is that close to Mike's heart rested those reassuring words of Bahá'u'lláh that were his life, his inspiration, his empowerment, and his total purpose in life.

As a product of the sixties, Mike had combined the qualities of his dynamic generation, which, at its best, sought fresh truths, with a firm determination to live a more meaningful life, and with a very early commitment to the Message of God for the day in which he lived.

Later I would write our Bahá'í friends, including those in Africa regarding Mike's passing:

"Mike might have had a foreboding that his life was drawing to a close. In a letter he wrote to me a few days before he passed he was commenting on my previous letter to him asking for his thoughts on his sister's plan to pioneer in the South to teach the Black people. He said that I must already know how he felt about pioneering for the Cause of God. He then referred me to P. 135 in Gleanings, the story of Ashraf and his mother. He said he had a feeling it was very relevant but he couldn't grasp the full significance of the story. He asked me to write back my thoughts on it. This passage brought me untold peace and strength in the difficult time that followed."

"'Call thou to mind the behavior of Ashraf's mother, whose son laid down his life in the Land of Za (Zanjan). He, most certainly, is in the seat of truth, in the presence of One Who is the Most Powerful, the Almighty.

'When the infidels, so unjustly, decided to put him to death, they sent and fetched his mother, that perchance she might admonish him, and induce him to recant his faith, and follow in the footsteps of them that have repudiated the truth of God, the Lord of all worlds.

'No sooner did she behold the face of her son, than she spoke to him such words as caused the hearts of the lovers of God, and beyond them those of the Concourse on high, to cry out and be sore pained with grief. Truly, thy Lord knoweth what My tongue speaketh. He Himself beareth witness to My words.

'And when addressing him she said: "My son, mine own son! Fail not to offer up thyself in the path of thy Lord. Beware that thou betray not thy faith in Him before Whose face have bowed down in adoration all who are in the heavens and all who are on the earth. Go thou straight on, O my son, and persevere in the path of the Lord, thy God. Haste thee to attain the presence of Him Who is the Well-Beloved of all worlds."

'On her be My blessings, and My mercy, and My praise, and My glory. I Myself shall atone for the loss of her son -- a son who now dwelleth within the tabernacle of My majesty and glory, and whose face beameth with a light that envelopeth with its radiance the Maids of Heaven in their celestial chambers, and beyond them the inmates of My Paradise, and the denizens of the Cities of Holiness. Were any eye to gaze on his face, he would exclaim: "Lo, this is no other than a noble angel!"'"

(Bahá'u'lláh, *Gleanings from the Writings of Bahá'u'lláh*, p. 134)

Mike's life had been a painful struggle in many ways, but toward the end it spoke of glorious fulfillment. He had completely surrendered himself to Bahá'u'lláh. Later I read in "The Seven Valleys":

"O My friend! Many a hound pursueth this gazelle of the desert of oneness; many a talon claweth at this thrush of the eternal garden. Pitiless ravens do lie in wait for this bird of the heavens of God, and the huntsman of envy stalketh this deer of the meadow of love.

O Shaykh! Make of thine effort a glass, perchance it may shelter this flame from the contrary winds; albeit this light doth long to be kindled in the lamp of the Lord, and to shine in the globe of the spirit. For the head raised up in the love of God will certainly fall by the sword, and the life that is kindled with longing will surely be sacrificed, and the heart which remembereth the Loved One will surely brim with blood." Bahá'u'lláh

I concluded my letter to our friends, "He had wanted so much to go on pilgrimage and had requested permission. The letter granting this for Nov. 10 arrived after his passing. Instead, Mike has made the ultimate pilgrimage to the Abhá Kingdom. We are very happy for him. And we feel so blessed to have had a son like him who was willing to give everything he had for the Cause of God."

Ama-t'ul-Bahá Ruhiyyih Khanum was in Africa at the time and wrote to us.

"We are gathered in the Sabri (Isobel and Hassan) home for the 19-Day Feast and I have read out loud at the end of the spiritual part the letter you sent to your Friends (dated Nov. 3rd) regarding Mike's death. It has uplifted all our hearts and renewed our joy in each other as believers in the Cause of

Bahá'u'lláh! Surely your son had an appointment to go to the next world – how wonderful he could hasten to keep that appointment with such a spirit of devotion to his Faith. May we all leave this world with a heart filled with love for the Cause as he did. May we all meet the death of our own near ones in the same spirit of faith you his family have shown! I send you my deepest love, in which all present join – many of them your old friends here, many of them new young Bahá'ís.   Ruhiyyih"

MY CLOSING WORDS TO THE YOUTH OF TODAY

....It is for you young Bahá'ís that I have written of my son and his spiritual journey of dedication, determination, and consecration, and to echo the Guardian's prophecy:

"youth can change the world!"....

www.ingramcontent.com/pod-product-compliance
Lightning Source LLC
Chambersburg PA
CBHW071325040426
42444CB00009B/2086